Puppy & Kitten Math

TELLING TIME
with PUPPIES
and
KITTENS

Patricia J. Murphy

Enslow Elementary

Contents

Words to Know

digital—Something that shows time or speed in numerals, or numbers.

hour—A unit of time. There are 24 hours in a day.

minute—A unit of time. There are 60 minutes in an hour.

What Time Is It?

We measure time in **minutes**, **hours**, and days. Days are filled with running, napping, and eating—especially if you are a puppy or kitten!

4

We look at clocks to tell the time.

Some clocks have faces.

Some do not.

Clocks with Faces

This clock has a face with numbers.
It has hands that move.
The hands show what time it is.
This is called a face clock.

These are the hands
of a face clock.
They show us the time.

Clocks without Faces

The numbers on this digital clock tell us the time.

This clock does not have a face.

It has numbers that change.

The numbers tell us what time it is.

This is called a **digital** clock.

Telling Time

To tell time, all you have to do is look.

1. Look at the minute hand (big hand).

    It is on the 12.

    This tells you it is a new hour.

2. Look at the hour hand (small hand).

    It is on the 3.

    This tells you what the hour is.

Telling Time Tip:
Sometimes we write time with
a : between the hour and minutes.
3 o'clock can be written as 3:00.

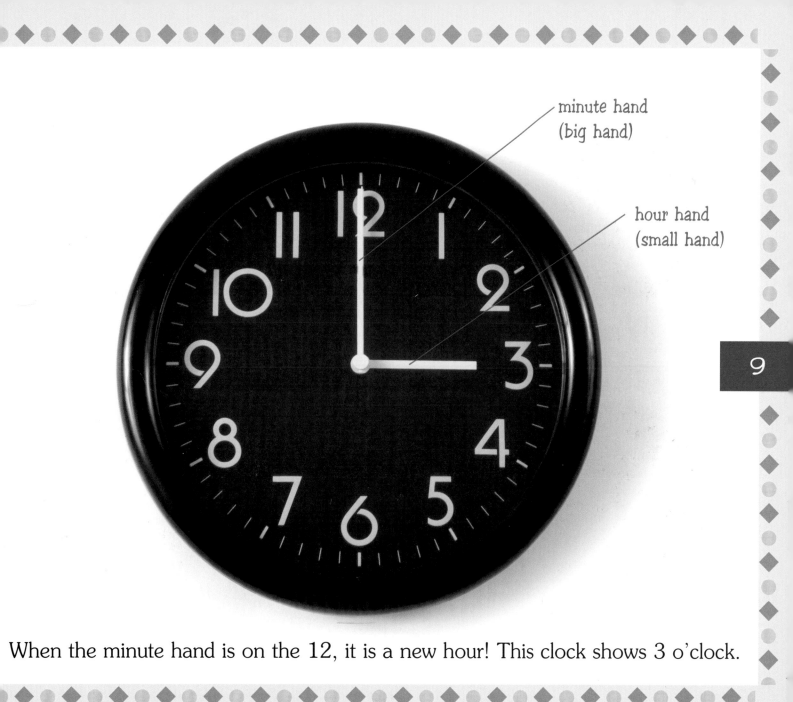

minute hand
(big hand)

hour hand
(small hand)

When the minute hand is on the 12, it is a new hour! This clock shows 3 o'clock.

Now you try. Tell time to the hour on these clocks.

12:00
12 o'clock
twelve o'clock

1:00
1 o'clock
one o'clock

2:00
2 o'clock
two o'clock

6:00
6 o'clock
six o'clock

7:00
7 o'clock
seven o'clock

8:00
8 o'clock
eight o'clock

3:00
3 o'clock
three o'clock

4:00
4 o'clock
four o'clock

5:00
5 o'clock
five o'clock

9:00
9 o'clock
nine o'clock

10:00
10 o'clock
ten o'clock

11:00
11 o'clock
eleven o'clock

Telling Time to the Half Hour

1. Look at the minute hand. It is on the 6. That means the hour is halfway over.

2. Look at the hour hand. It is between the 9 and 10. That means it is halfway between 9:00 and 10:00. This clock shows 9:30.

Telling Time Tip: There are 60 minutes in an hour. There are 30 minutes in a half hour.

The minute hand has gone HALFWAY around the clock.

Now it's your turn. Tell time to the half hour on these clocks.

12:30
twelve-thirty

1:30
one-thirty

2:30
two-thirty

3:30
three-thirty

4:30
four-thirty

5:30
five-thirty

6:30
six-thirty

7:30
seven-thirty

8:30
eight-thirty

9:30
nine-thirty

10:30
ten-thirty

11:30
eleven-thirty

Telling Time with Digital Clocks

Look at the hour.   Look at the minutes.

This clock shows 6:30.

We call this time: **six-thirty**.   We write this time: **6:30**.

Now you try! Tell time on these clocks.

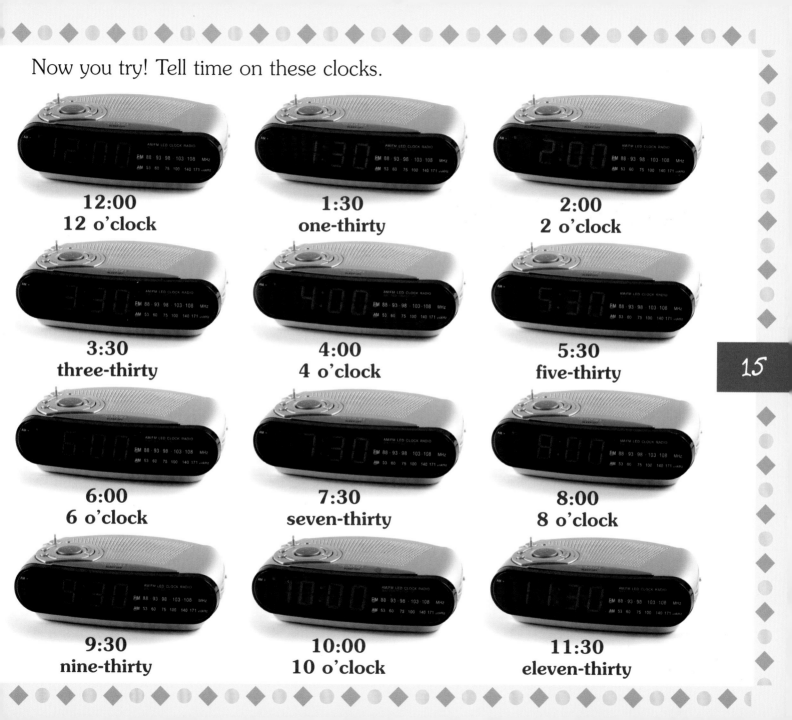

12:00
12 o'clock

1:30
one-thirty

2:00
2 o'clock

3:30
three-thirty

4:00
4 o'clock

5:30
five-thirty

6:00
6 o'clock

7:30
seven-thirty

8:00
8 o'clock

9:30
nine-thirty

10:00
10 o'clock

11:30
eleven-thirty

Time for Puppies and Kittens

We write: **8:00**
We say: **"8 o'clock"**

Puppies wake up.

Good morning, pup!

We write: **9:00**
We say: **"9 o'clock"**

Telling Time Tip: We use A.M. for morning hours. You might see 9 o'clock in the morning written as 9:00 A.M.

Puppies eat breakfast. Yum!

We write: **10:00**
We say: **"10 o'clock"**

Kittens stay inside.
Some chase balls.
Others hide.

We write: **11:30**
We say: **"eleven-thirty"**

Splish. Splash.
Puppy needs a bath.

19

We write: **12:00**
We say: **"12 o'clock,"** or **"noon"**

Puppies and kittens eat lunch.
How can they eat so much?

We write: **12:30**
We say: **"twelve-thirty"**

It's time for a nap.

Puppies sleep.

Kittens dream of snacks.

Telling Time Tip: We use P.M. for afternoon and night hours. You may see 12:30 in the afternoon written as 12:30 P.M.

We write: **2:00**
We say: **"2 o'clock"**

Some puppies run around.

We write: **3:30**
We say: **"three-thirty"**

Some kittens go to the playground.

We write: **5:00**
We say: **"5 o'clock"**

Dinnertime!
Puppies and kittens
eat every bite.

We write: **6:30**
We say: **"six-thirty"**

Grab a brush or two.
It is time for puppies
and kittens to groom.

We write: **7:30**
We say: **"seven-thirty"**

Time for one last trip outside!
Some puppies bark at noises.
Others chase butterflies.

WOOF!

We write: **8:00**
We say: **"8 o'clock"**

It's time for bed. Puppies and kittens rest their sleepy heads. Sweet dreams.

ZZZZZZZ...

Looking Back

We can tell time using two different clocks:

number — minute hand

face — hour hand

face clock

hour

minutes

digital clock

We can tell time to the hour:

12:00 1:00 2:00 3:00 4:00 5:00

6:00 7:00 8:00 9:00 10:00 11:00

We can tell time to the half hour:

12:30   1:30   2:30   3:30   4:30   5:30

6:30   7:30   8:30   9:30   10:30   11:30

We can write time in different ways: 7 o'clock, 7:00.

Time for Activities

Keep a Log of Your Day

Write down the things you do and the times you do them. Start with the time you get up until the time you go to bed. Draw clocks showing the times to the hour and half hour. Share your log with a friend.

Make a Clock Collage

Cut out pictures of clocks from magazines and newspapers. Glue them on a piece of paper and let it dry. Next, write the times the clocks show below them. Then, put up your clock picture for everyone to see.

Learn More

Books

Koscielniak, Bruce. *About Time: A First Look at Time and Clocks*. Boston: Houghton Mifflin, 2004.

Murphy, Patricia J. *A Day*. Manakato, Minn.: Capstone Press, 2005.

Murphy, Stuart J. *It's about Time!* New York: HarperCollins, 2005.

Web Sites

GoKidding
<http://www.gokidding.com/>

The Sun: Man's Friend & Foe—Time
<http://library.thinkquest.org/15215/Friend/time.html>

What Time Is It?
<http://www.primarygames.com/time/start.htm>

Index

Series Math Consultant
Eileen Fernández, Ph.D.
Associate Professor, Mathematics Education
Montclair State University
Montclair, NJ

Series Literacy Consultant
Allan A. De Fina, Ph.D.
Past President of the New Jersey Reading Association
Professor, Department of Literacy Education
New Jersey City University
Jersey City, NJ

For Mrs. Farmer

Acknowledgments: The author thanks Arlington Heights School District #25, in Arlington Heights, IL, and Lake Forest School District #67, in Lake Forest, IL, for their assistance in the research of this book.

Enslow Elementary, an imprint of Enslow Publishers, Inc.
Enslow Elementary® is a registered trademark of Enslow Publishers, Inc.

Library of Congress Cataloging-in-Publication Data

Murphy, Patricia J., 1963–
    Telling time with puppies and kittens / by Patricia J. Murphy.
        p. cm. — (Puppy and kitten math)
    Includes bibliographical references and index.
    ISBN-13: 978-0-7660-2728-2
    ISBN-10: 0-7660-2728-7
    1. Time—Juvenile literature. I. Title.
    QB209.5.M86 2007
    529—dc22
                                                        2006004874

Printed in the United States of America

10 9 8 7 6 5 4 3 2 1

Photo credits: © age fotostock/SuperStock, p. 26 (right); ©Alison Barnes Martin/Masterfile, p. 16; © 2004 Brand X Pictures, p. 24; Carolinehenri/Dreamstime.com, p. 20 (kitten); Enslow Publishers, Inc., all clocks; Hemera Technologies, p. 4 (cats in bed); iStock, pp. 3 (puppies), 4 (with ball), 14, 25 (brush), 31 (puppy); iStockphoto.com/Justin Horrocks, p. 28; Jane Burton/Photo Researchers, Inc., pp. 5, 26 (left), 27; Kati1313/Dreamstime, p. 25 (kitten); Shutterstock, pp. 1, 3 (kitten), 4 (largest puppy), 8, 12, 17, 18, 19, 20 (puppy), 21, 23, 25 (puppy), 30, 31 (kitten); SuperStock, Inc./Superstock, p. 29; Troy Wuelfing/ Dreamstime, p. 22; Warren Photographic, p. 4 (kitten).

Cover photo: © Warren Photographic

Enslow Elementary
an imprint of
Enslow Publishers, Inc.
40 Industrial Road
Box 398
Berkeley Heights, NJ 07922
USA
http://www.enslow.com